The Human Side

The Human Side

ARVILLA FEE
Foreword by Christopher Bays

RESOURCE *Publications* · Eugene, Oregon

THE HUMAN SIDE

Copyright © 2022 Arvilla Fee. All rights reserved. Except for brief quotations in critical publications or reviews, no part of this book may be reproduced in any manner without prior written permission from the publisher. Write: Permissions, Wipf and Stock Publishers, 199 W. 8th Ave., Suite 3, Eugene, OR 97401.

Resource Publications
An Imprint of Wipf and Stock Publishers
199 W. 8th Ave., Suite 3
Eugene, OR 97401

www.wipfandstock.com

PAPERBACK ISBN: 978-1-6667-6079-8
HARDCOVER ISBN: 978-1-6667-6080-4
EBOOK ISBN: 978-1-6667-6081-1

11/28/22

I dedicate this book first to God, who gave me the wondrous ability to turn words into art. Next, to my mom, Shirley; my sister, Carla; and my daughter, Jennica—my brightest stars and biggest fans. To my husband, Jamie who is my love of almost twenty-one years, is incredibly selfless, and often entertains our little one, so I can spend an exorbitant amount of time writing in the evenings. To my brother, Rob, who has supported my writing and has read nearly every poem I've ever written; he appreciates the power of the pen. To my dad, Ray who has encouraged me to succeed in all my endeavors. To my dear friend, Brian, who has also spent countless hours helping me while I immersed myself in my poetry. To the rest of my lovely children (bio and adopted), their significant others, and the sweetest little granddaughter in the world: Kara, Kyle, Stephanie, Embree, Armoni, Kaitlyn, Alec, and D'Andre (love you all so much!). To a former student and friend, Makayla, to whom I've dedicated a poem in this book (Stay fierce, love!). To another former student, Nicole, to whom I've also dedicated a poem in this book (I'm proud of you. Go teach the next generation for me!) To my sweet dog, Rio, who faithfully sits beside me no matter how many hours I spend on the computer! To my professors and colleagues at Auburn University of Montgomery who have enriched my life in everlasting ways. And last, but not least, I'd like to offer a special thanks to one of the best professors of creative writing on the planet, Christopher Bays, who taught me the exquisite art of haibun.

CONTENTS

Foreword by Christopher Bays   xi
Preface   xiii

Part I | The Addicted

An Addict's Siren	3
The Elephant in the Room	5
A Jagged Scar	7
Life with an Addict	8
Make Me a Monster	11
Moth to Flame	12
Sister's Overdose Undone	14
Sometimes War	15
Speak of the Dead	16
When the Top Stopped	18
Wrong Side of the Tracks	21

Part II | The Abused

Bare	25
Handle with Care	28
Hurt	29
Inside the Globe	30
It Was That May	32
Kalamata Olives	34
No Strings Attached	36
Portrait of a Buried Self	37
Rearview	39
Tinseltown	40
Unmentionables	41
Your True Colors	43

CONTENTS

Part III | The Forgotten

45th Street Gallery	47
Angels Unaware	48
Between the Bars	49
Catch and Release	50
Church Bells	51
Church Door Shadow	54
The Court of Cats	55
Every Day is Amber	57
He Had a Name	58
The Last of Their Kind	60
Left Behind	63
Loneliness	64
Miss Gertie Next Door	66
The Nature of One	67
No Place to Call Home	68
Shallows	70
Shut Ins	71
Things We Don't Mention	72
Through the Lens	75
Vagrant	77
Write for Me	79

Part IV | The Grieved

Ancient Stories	85
"Atlas Shrugged"	86
Behind the Smile	88
Catacombs	89
Harmonious Cacophony	91
The Hollow	93
Interlude	94
Just for the Night	96
A Lifetime of Ellipses	97
Revelation: Your Mom Has a Brain Tumor	98
Rows Not Planted	100

Selling Grief	101
Table for One	102
Talking to God	103
Transient	105
Two Peas in Different Pods	106
Wasting Disease	108
Wear Your Best Black	109
When My Brain Was a Bucket	110
Where the Lost Things Go	111
Whiffler	113

Part V | The Resilient

Beyond Getting Even	117
Close the Door on Your Way Out	120
Conquering Mountains	121
Eulogy to My Former Self	123
Excuse Me	124
Failure to Fail	126
Flight	128
Friend Request	129
Give My Regards	131
The Human Story	132
I Believe	134
In My Alternate Life	136
Inside Ingredient	137
Looking for the Spirit	138
Moxie	140
Purple Hearts Still Bleed	142
Reinvention	146
The Sayer of Grace	147
Second Spring	148
Shoeshine in Tokyo	149
Squeezing Those Lemons	150
Things You Carried	151
Watershed Moment	152
"You are Your Best Thing"	153

Contents

You're Sitting on the Tracks   155
You Wanted Me to Spare Your Feelings   156
Zenith   157

Acknowledgments   159
About the Author   161

FOREWORD

What you hold in your hands is not a collection of esoteric musings. It is not a maze of puzzles to decipher—as some 21st century poetry demands of readers. It is, instead, a book that is as approachable as a close friend—a friend who has a gift for sharing with you experiences, both emotional and transformative, that are based on things of this world and beyond.

Expect to see lines that sweep you in one breath from fried chicken to angelic wings. Expect unusual words, such as "scritch," that are like special desserts made just for you. Expect to find people struggling with addiction, abuse, and loss. Will they be able to rise from their infernos? Are there still heroes or have they been forgotten? How will Arvilla Fee, the poet, rise above the cragged path of the past?

By journeying through the entire collection, you may find, as I have, that Arvilla's musical, image-rich poems unfold into each other and become more profound when seen as a whole. Yes, individual poems will leave you breathless, but the collection will make you feel, as the title of the book states, the human side.

Arvilla's book is accessible and substantive. I hope you enjoy reading it as much as I have.

CHRISTOPHER BAYS
Professor of English, Clark State College
Author of the poetry book, "Lost on the Edge of Suburbia"

PREFACE

People often ask me where I get my ideas or inspiration for poetry. The short answer is *life*. The longer (and more complex) answer is an overactive brain that is supercharged with creativity and constantly seeks to put words to experiences, observations, and emotions. While I've written most of the poems in *The Human Side* over the past four years, the "inspiration," painful as it was at times, has spanned more than three decades. Granted, these pieces are not "truth" in the sense that this collection aspires to be a memoir, but rather artistic expressions that seek to address the commonality of human suffering and resilience.

I write to give a voice to those who can't find adequate words: to those who have suffered a miscarriage, been through a painful divorce, watched a loved one deteriorate with Alzheimer's, suffered abuse at the hands of a loved one, lost a loved one to drug or alcohol abuse, dealt with wayward children, or endured toxic relationships. I also write for the underdog—for those society pretends not to see. For the lonely widow, for the outcast teen, for the single mom, for the homeless person on the street, for the poor, for the addict, and for the bereft.

Some of my best pieces literally come to me in the middle of the night. I keep a notebook and pen beside my bed, and I often find myself scribbling by the faint light of the nightlight in the bathroom as words tumble through my head like socks in a dryer. My husband will sometimes wake up and say, "What are you doing?" My answer is, "Writing stuff down." He's learned this is my normal. I've also written down ideas while stopped at traffic lights! I keep ongoing lists of cool words, odd phrases and expressions, and meaningful quotes from books. My mantra: never waste a good idea. If I could carry words in my pockets, I would.

To anyone who aspires to write, I say, "Do it!" You'll need a few tools in your belt, a little bit of time, and a lot of patience, but allow

Preface

ideas to flow through you. You might be surprised! Having spent over twenty years as an English teacher, I give my students these tips when writing:

1. *Show, don't tell.* Avoid the use of vague descriptions. Don't say someone is "happy." Say, "Kaitlyn jumped to her feet and clapped her hands together, her face glowing."
2. *Less is more.* While this might seem a contradiction of the first point, it is not. Choose power words, action words, words that concretely express the idea without unnecessary fluff. Haiku and Haibun are both perfect constructs for learning this trick.
3. *Use a thesaurus.* There are literally millions of words that go unused because we tend to default to an ordinary word. Be bold. Don't be afraid to say, "She gazed out of the window, her melancholy mood draped like a wet blanket over her frail shoulders."

It is my hope and prayer that each reader who turns the pages of this book receives *something*. If nothing else, I hope my readers (even those who do not fancy themselves poetry lovers) say, "This is what I've been looking for. She gets it! She gets me!"

PART I

The Addicted

PART I | THE ADDICTED

AN ADDICT'S SIREN

You knew me;
you called my name
with that come hither
wink of an eye
finger waggling,
lips pouting;
you knew
what I would do—
that you'd be my
undoing,
knew I couldn't
look away
from the snake
charmer's charm
or the arm that
trapped me,
enraptured me,
pushing poison
through my veins,
sweet poison—
the elixir of gods
or of demons,
I don't know which,
It's only a fix.
You knew my blood
cried for it—
that I'd die for it,
so, you stand on the

The Human Side

cliff and sing,
God knows I have
nothing to bring
except a body
marked, spent,
hell-bent on
extinction.
Throw me over
the brink; I'll drown
in the sea for you,
sink to the bottom
my siren, my muse.

PART I | THE ADDICTED

THE ELEPHANT IN THE ROOM

A 4th of July picnic brings in the family and homemade cherry pies and Mamaw's lemonade. Long-lost cousins are euphoric and run screaming through the wide front lawn as if they had been cooped up in a room until that very moment and then released like puppies out of a kennel. But certain family members, who showed up two hours late, aren't quite as. . .energetic. Everyone notices their eyes, dilated pupils, the slight slurring of words, and the way their heads loll to one side when trying to sit in a chair. Yet no one mentions any of this as they continue to talk and eat watermelon, with juice dripping from their chins. The late arrivals have explained that they are tired, have headaches, stomach aches and the like. Everyone nods and coos sympathetically as if these excuses are perfectly plausible. . .while one sister's head seems to snap off at a rakish angle from her shoulders, her mouth gaping, emitting rhythmic snores. I watch the faces in the semicircle, but everyone continues telling jokes as if the three incapacitated siblings, who are all snoring now, are perfectly normal humans— as if none of them have injected themselves with a liquid catalyst just so they can get through the day without clawing their skin off. I start to say

The Human Side

something, but I know my words will hold water like a sieve. It is what it is—another holiday that will be swept under the proverbial rug even before darkness explodes with the first fireworks shot over the hill.

PART I | THE ADDICTED

A JAGGED SCAR

runs the length of her
left cheek,
left there by betrayal,
although she was paid
in copper tubing,
which she was able to trade
for a one-inch square
of dreamless powder.

A jagged scar
runs the length of her
heart,
left there by parents,
ex-husbands, county courts;
she has nothing left to trade;
shivers scrape her skin;
the cell bunk unforgiving.

LIFE WITH AN ADDICT

Arms folded,
darkness my only blanket—
alone on the couch...
    waiting,
    breathing,
    anticipating
    the worst.

The door creaks;
I must oil that—
but no, the creak
announces his entrance:
    sneaky,
    guilt-ridden
    tread of boots.

I could ask,
"Where have you been?"
But, oh, the futility!
That one question
produces
    lies,
    denials,
    well-worn excuses
    I've heard before.

I flick on the lamp,
startling him

into a lopsided grin,
a grin that doesn't
quite reach
eyes that are
        bleary,
        dilated,
        stoned.

In the stilted silence,
I stand,
and he moves
to hug me;
a heroin hug,
that's what I call it,
chemically produced
emotion—
        empty,
        meaningless,
        dead.
For even with
his arms around me,
I know
the minute he comes down,
he would steal
        my watch,
        my computer,
        his grandma's false teeth
        to get high again.

"Go to bed,"
I say.
And he nods.

The Human Side

He knows,
somewhere
in that scrambled brain,
that he needs
help—

    and that we will talk
    about all of this again
    tomorrow.

PART I | THE ADDICTED

MAKE ME A MONSTER

strip me—
search cavities
drape me
in cotton-poly blend

lead me
through the gauntlet
lock me
in my 6 by 8 hell

leave me
to add my stains
ignore me,
my throat unzipped with screams

tell me
I'm just an addict
treat me
with razor wire and clubs

blame me
when I am free
only to return
as the monster
you made me.

THE HUMAN SIDE

MOTH TO FLAME

Dumpsters ripe with rot

    fur-covered ribs

pad lightly around potholes

    filled with rain

searching

all are searching

    for that fix

    scratch for the itch

a flame—single point of light

in the inky night

    powder melts on a spoon

    rubber band reveals

    a blood-rich vein

suck from the syringe

like a nursing infant

    can't look away

        from desire or death.

SISTER'S OVERDOSE UNDONE

Color rushes back to her lips,
placid blue surrendering to rosy
pink; the paramedics backstep
in sync, automatons without
purpose, return to the station in
silence. Rubber band snaps off
her arm, liquid heroin spurts like
blood from her veins: thump, thump
thump, thump; her heart returns
to its native beat. The liquid moves
from spoon to needle then puffs like
a dragon (all smoke, no fire) back
into the one-inch square of foil.
Lighter and spoon are nested in
her purse like vipers with fangs
removed. Her hands are steady
as she clutches the sink. Warm
brown eyes return her gaze in the
mirror. She unlocks the bathroom
door and breezes into the living
room. *I'm ready to go to rehab,*
she announces. I grab my keys.

SOMETIMES WAR

Sometimes there are no medals,
no spent cartridges
no acrid smell of powder in the air;
sometimes war is fought with
the distant wailing of sirens
and lights that blaze red against
the inky sky. . .
by gloved hands that rip open
a package of Narcan
and plunge it into the legs
of our dying sons and daughters
who were felled by an enemy
that marches
in little plastic bags,
bullets that shoot from the end
of syringes
and storm the blood.
Sometimes the dead are returned
to life
and sometimes soldiers
remove their masks to cry.

The Human Side

SPEAK OF THE DEAD

She could light up a room;
everyone loved her;

she had an infectious laugh;
she loved children;

everyone wanted
to be her friend...

Sometimes I think people
grab eulogies out of cans—

just pop that top off
and pull it out!

Not saying these words
aren't true (necessarily)

but what *else* is in that can?

Will anyone dare say
that she made bad choices,

that she liked to get high,
and smoked two packs a day?

No one will.

Nor will anyone mention
that she could have lived

really lived—
had it not been for opioids

and meth
and booze

and the pain in her back
that drove her to all the above.

No one will say
that her worthless baby daddy
gave her the hit
that turned her lips blue

or that her kids
are now scarred for life,

that they might turn out
to be addicts too,

and the cycle will continue
like a rogue merry-go-round,

the same music playing
over—and over—and over.

Speak of the *dead*.

THE HUMAN SIDE

WHEN THE TOP STOPPED

I remember you walking out the door,
wanting that Mt. Dew and cigarette a.m. rush,
but I made you come back inside and take a woman's daily
with your sweet rolls and bacon.
You laughed and called me bossy, and I agreed—
but I wasn't going to let you smoke breakfast!
Your eyes were clear back then as you searched for jobs
and flashed your dreams like a card trick;
you were a good pretender, the perfect cultured counterfeit—
but your three children witnessed the naked truth.
They sat outside on a curb as you drove by, and you didn't call out
to them or wave; you didn't know them;
            you didn't know them!
You'd wake them up for school on days they didn't have school,
shouting at them to hurry; the benders became more frequent,
often melding days together in a manic frenzy—no sleep, no food.
It was agonizing to watch your skin sagging into your wasted,
washed-out frame of bones and unkempt hair;
trips to the emergency room were called
"low potassium," but no banana—
            no banana could fix that!
How often I wanted to reach inside your chemical strangled brain
and
yank out (with both hands)—*like one would yank the orange guts out of*
a Halloween pumpkin—that damn dependency that kept you chained
to that two-bit town with its two-bit dealers and that gas station

where people made trades and drank Polar Pops,
>   grinning with nicotine teeth.
But I couldn't do that; no one could; so, we watched you spin and spin
until you spun yourself into jail over a stupid Walmart shopping cart full
of unpaid merchandise that you decided to trundle out the door.
You were safe, for the moment, safe with your itchy skin and the bugs
of withdrawal crawling all over you.
Keep her there, we screamed at your mother; *keep her there—*
>   But she didn't listen.
>   She never freaking listened!
Bailed out, you made calls to *rehab centers*—in hushed tones behind
closed doors, "Can you get me something?"
The person who was supposed to love you the *most* took wheels, made deals,
and slid sly hands into your back pocket while hugging.
>   *No diff*erent than when Judas
>   kissed t*he Christ.*
A ribbonless package of back-alley powder: your crutch, your oblivion,
your existential exit—*stage right* behind the curtain;
>   you slipped behind the curtain!
No banging on the bathroom door could make you open it;
the EMTs burst through. . .28, 29, 30—breath, breath. . .28, 29, 30. .
but no life resurrected those blue lips that once laughed and spoke
with fizzy optimism about the future.
So, we sat at your funeral, numb with shock and sorrow,
casting unmitigated barbs of anger at that pea-brained
bastard on the front row, his arms around your children,
full of snot and tears—

The Human Side

    tortured, we hoped, with the punishing guilt of owning the hands
        that tipped the top
            on its side.

PART I | *THE ADDICTED*

WRONG SIDE OF THE TRACKS

"Guuurrl"—if you knew Dana, that was how she began almost every story. And she didn't just tell a story with words; her hands waved in a theatrical blur, until she fell over on the floor, laughing. No matter what family function we were having, Dana always seemed to be at the center. And Lord help us if Dana cocked her head sideways like a puppy when confronted with a piece of mind-bending trivia. "Hold on—say what?" Like the time we had to explain that a prime minister wasn't part of the Catholic church. No one could be in a hurry to leave either. A person didn't dare walk away from Dana without getting at least three hugs and a dozen I-love-you's. And that amount tripled for the kids.

We didn't talk about her demons. There were a few odd visits—with dilated pupils and lapses in conversations. Maybe an occasional trip to the ER—low potassium levels, we were told. But she seemed to have them under control. Until that one night, and all we hear now are the words of the EMTs: *nothing we could do.*

no hand on the glass—
the train pulls away
from the station

PART II

The Abused

BARE

branches stripped of color
sheathed in ice

scritch against the window
exposed to the wind

offering shelter to no one,
naked alone

like the girl lying face down
in a moldy motel room

without a stitch of dignity
atop the polyester cover

stained with many a sin
not yet washed clean

it was only one drink,
a mixed drink at that—

one of those fruity
4% alcohol things,

but no one witnessed
Winter's sleight of hand

The Human Side

snowflakes dissolving
in the ice-filled glass

chink, chink

and the North wind
blew down her throat

stripped every color:
blue jeans, t-shirt, bra

naked alone
she could tell no one

who was there to tell?
she didn't know his name

shame shivered through
her paralyzed limbs;

she'd never seen spring
again, she thought,

but somehow time
thawed the skin

and tiny green buds
grew at the ends

of each of her fingertips
and she stared at them

for ages, almost afraid
to breathe

for fear they would
suffer a fatal frost

so, she kept them as
close as her heartbeat

until they unfurled
into courageous leaves

and grew strong *enough*

to absorb both wind and rain

THE HUMAN SIDE

HANDLE WITH CARE

dropped—
glass shatters
spraying shards;

fragments
bleed into
hardwood floors;

chin up
says a friend
who's intact;

I comb
through edges
for my heart;

a mouse
carries it off
to his hole.

PART II | THE ABUSED

HURT

fist connects
with mirror

glass shatters

face fragments
into a Picasso

blood drips
leaves spots

on the sink

sticks and stones
may break my bones

but words
cut me.

INSIDE THE GLOBE

Snow gently falls,
like feathers
on a house
that is seductively
pleasant,
the kind featured
in the glossy pages
of high-dollar magazines.

There is no sound
behind each lit window,
save for the distant
tinkling of notes
stilted,
as though a key,
half-turned,
is growing weary.

We know nothing
of the people
inside,
and even if we
shake it again,
we'd only see
the snow
the snow
the snow.

PART II | THE ABUSED

But drop the globe;
yes, drop it.
Let it shatter;
let the glass
smack the floor
and the water
make a puddle
around your feet.

Let the house
crack open.
Expose the rooms,
the overflowing
ash trays,
the rings
on the coffee table—
callous imprints
of whiskey-sat-too-long.
Expose the bruises
and the apologies
and the mascara trails
on satin-covered
pillows.

There really never was
any snow.

The Human Side

IT WAS THAT MAY

the cicadas came crawling
out of the ground—Brood X
Gramps said, the kind that
only emerges every 17 years.

He was smart like that, even
though my mom and her Flavor-
of-the-Month thought Gramps
to be an Alzheimered old fool.

It was that May when I was
nursing my rib cage from a punch
Mr. Flavor let fly when I told him
to get his dumb ass outta my room.

It was that May Gramps coughed
and wheezed out an apology
about his train getting ready
to leave the station, and I buried

against his old flannel, inhaling
scents of Dial soap and tobacco.
I told him I still needed my knight;
he patted the back of my head.

It was that May the cicadas shed
their exoskeletons and Gramps

told me I'd have to shed mine too
and learn how to use my wings.

He rifled his hair with his fingers
until it stuck up like white caps
on the lake and peered over his
bifocals, flashing his crooked smile.

It was that May Gramps left me,
and I unraveled like a knit sweater
with a pulled string, snot and tears
bereaving my face until it stung.

It was six weeks after that May
I burrowed with the larvae, feeding
on fluids sucked from the roots of trees
comfortable with anonymity
among millions of my kind.

KALAMATA OLIVES

Oh, how patiently I waited;
I dared not pick them green.
Time and sun transformed
each almond-shaped bulb
into a rich dark brown, like
that of a fresh bruise.

I touch my cheek, gingerly
then place each olive into a
jar of weak brine mixed
with wine vinegar. I add a
layer of olive oil, followed
by delicate slices of lemon
as thin as eyelids.

My eyelids are not thin
but are encrusted with
salt, thicker than the olive
brine—and I wonder
what it would be like,

to be nestled into a jar and
tucked away for months in
the back of a dark pantry,
juices slowly seeping beneath
my skin into the deepest parts

of me— knowing that
someday I will emerge,
debittered.

NO STRINGS ATTACHED

Your manic grin behind the brick façade, behind the curtains where you played your sick game—you jerked and pulled, commandeered each of my twisted limbs for the drama you designed. But little did you know how resourceful I was with scissors! One bone-chilling day in December when you flexed your fingers and snatched the crossbar that once tied me to your temper, I was gone!

I'm a real girl now
the one who got
away

PORTRAIT OF A BURIED SELF

She was the mirror without a reflection
that steamed from the heat of her bath.
She was the bath that reddened her skin
before toweling dry, and
She was the towel that dabbed at tears
he'd produced with a word, and
She was a word in a jar.

She was the jar that he placed on a shelf
meant to be seen by his guests, and
She was a guest framed in a dress with
bangles on her arm, and
She was an arm on his side who nodded
and graciously smiled.
She was a smile with pale lipstick.

She was the lipstick that left marks
on the wine glass, the one drink she
was allowed to have, and
She was the drink when he was thirsty
and smothered her with his body.
She was the body in a church where
vows were spoken.

She was the vow that chained her
to the gold band upon her finger,

The Human Side

She was the band that circled and circled
without end, and
She was the end of herself.

She was the mirror without a reflection.

PART II | THE ABUSED

REARVIEW

I abandon the search for my ego and
pack bruises into a suitcase beneath
garments that witnessed my descent
into despair—

shirts now ripped and torn by one who
promised to be kind. He must have
winked at God, crossed devil fingers
behind his back.

Full tank of gas, the car rolls down
the driveway, swallowed whole by a
starless night. I won't look back.
I'm not Lot's wife.

THE HUMAN SIDE

TINSELTOWN

You know your lines, and I know mine. We've rehearsed these parts over and over—haven't we? We know when to exit and when to enter. "Darling, that dress looks splendid!" you say. I glow under the white lights and tilt my head, just so. "Why, thank you." Your clothes hang on the right side of the closet; mine hang on the left. You take your coffee with one teaspoon of creamer. One teaspoon, and not a drop more. I know to turn and smile when you put your hand on the small of my back. A director would be pleased, I think. Maybe. Or maybe he would tell us to relax our shoulders a bit—to act more naturally. I think about this as we sit down to dinner—others ebbing and flowing around us, taking our order, filling our drinks. The napkins are pristine; the silverware arranged impeccably. Just like us. But I want to tell the woman whose gaze skitters past me to land on you, practically begging you to meet her lust-filled eyes, what lies beyond the props.

counterfeit smile
cosmetics cover
a multitude of sins

UNMENTIONABLES

She's alive;
they tell her that's the most important
thing. She didn't die.

But part of her did—
the part that smeared blood between her
legs, covered her back with bruises.

They bring a rape kit
into the room, and she shivers violently
as if her ribs are rubber bands.

More photographs. Questions.
You didn't touch anything? Didn't shower?
No. She'd only pulled her hair

up into a bun again. The way it was—
before. There will always be that line now,
Before. After.

After stings her face with a fierce blush
when the officer asks her what she'd been
wearing. How much

she'd had to drink. I didn't die, she thinks.
I lived so I could explain I was wearing black
slacks, drinking club soda.

The Human Side

She wants to dress now. Not in clothes, but in pride—dignity. In the absence of those, she will remain naked the rest of her life.

YOUR TRUE COLORS

You're quite the
chameleon

aren't you—

blending seamlessly from
corporate world

to amiable guy
sitting on a bar stool

to dedicated saint with
communion melting
on his tongue.

You sit as easily in
a suit as you do in
jeans and a polo.

You can arrange
your face to please
boss man,
barmaid,
and priest.

And yet—no one
knows you

The Human Side

like I do.

There's one color others
do not see.

The inky blackness
that permeates your
pores

the minute you step
through the door

of our home. It's
only there that
you cease to
radiate

the multi shades of
iridescent blues
tranquil greens and
noble purples.

Only I can see you,

and only I know
you are not a true
chameleon.

PART III

The Forgotten

PART III | THE FORGOTTEN

45TH STREET GALLERY

Half-baked moon, burn
marks from cigarettes
kicking rusty cans—

streets fraught with rejection,
canvas sneakers pinching
restless dirty feet

untouchable glazed donuts;
you don't have to pay for
reflections in glass windows

a pigeon waits beneath a sign
don't feed the pigeons—but
no one follows the rules.

The Human Side

ANGELS UNAWARE

I barely glance at the older woman parked next to me. Got groceries, check. Now to get gas, check. Then finish laundry at home. My mind races ahead like horses, and I, the driver, have lost the reins. Putting my car in reverse, I begin backing out of my space. The older woman, who had been in one of those wheelchair carts, is attempting to lift her groceries out of the basket into her backseat. *Stop.* That is definitely not my brain. I pull back into my space and get out. "Would you like some help?" I ask her. "Oh, that would be so nice," she says. I help her transfer the bags, one-by-one. "You know," she says, as I reach for the last bag, "I lost my husband a year ago, and now no one sees me." My heart contracts painfully in my chest. Guilty. I had almost been guilty. "I see you," I say softly. The lines crinkle around her eyes as she smiles up at me. Back in my car, I hold onto the steering wheel for several seconds—just breathing, just being.

rearview mirror
gossamer wings
trick of the light

PART III | THE FORGOTTEN

BETWEEN THE BARS

Streets deserted, save for boney frames of fur poking damp noses into dumpsters. A lone figure emerges from the alley, feeling eyes on the back of his hooded head; his Adam's apple bobs as he swallows. He failed school, but he can't fail this. The gang plays for keeps. Hands trembling, he's in the car in under six seconds. Hot wires bring it to life; he presses the pedal. Two blocks later, red and blue in the rearview. He pulls to the curb. Officer: *do you know why I pulled you over?* He says nothing. Officer: *step out of the car.* He's booked at the station. Fingerprints, the flash of a camera: left, right. Orange clothes dwarf his too-thin, too-black frame. He holds the string of his pants between clenched fists. The eyes in the alley will not search for him—no one will, except a disgruntled gray lawyer with a 5 o'clock shadow, claiming the State is flat broke.

human flesh
pressing together
Lady Justice sleeps

CATCH AND RELEASE

So, yeah, it don't matter what they say about those forever homes; they don't exist. Who came up with that anyway? Some glass-is-half-full man in a golf polo who smiles at you behind wirerimmed glasses while making scratchy notations on his chart? What I wouldn't give to snatch one of those pages and see what they say about me. Probably a bunch of boxes. *Stayed out too late.* Check. *Sass-mouthed the teacher.* Check. *Lifted some cigarettes from the man of the house.* Check. Whatever. I ain't staying. I could make my bed every day and sprinkle it with fairy dust, but nobody wants me. They tell me I should consider my future—that I'm about to age out of the system. I tell them all to go to hell cause I got big plans that I ain't telling.

silver shines pretty
in the mouths
of fools

PART III | THE FORGOTTEN

CHURCH BELLS

The pop-pop
of gunshots,
another man sprawled
in oil-slicked streets.
A junkie shooting up
on the corner
of Fifth and Main;
he'll sink beneath
the heroin sea
and swim euphorically
until sunrise.

Do you hear
the church bells
ringing?

A homeless woman
begging,
shoeless feet
and matted hair –
where did she once
belong?
Candy bars
slipped into pockets,
a hooded teen
just released
from juvie.

The Human Side

Do you hear
the church bells
ringing?

A car approaches;
the young lady
in a leopard-print
states her price.
She settles down
in leather,
letting the heat
warm her legs.
The man grins,
a hunter proud
of easy prey.
Do you hear
the church bells
ringing?

Smudgy faces,
not a pedicure
in sight.
Empty eyes
cast downward
because looking up
requires hope.
A knife means life
—or death,
depends on which end
of the blade
one is facing.

Some will glance
bitterly—or longingly
at the imposing stone
structure.
The one with the belfry
and the ten-foot door
where the priest
warmly greets
parishioners who wear
cuff links
and well-pressed skirts.

Do you hear
the church bells
ringing?

CHURCH DOOR SHADOW

I hold my daughter's little hand in mine even though the bleached Italian sun generates heatwaves from the afternoon sidewalk, making us sticky with sweat. I know we look like tourists, the way we gawk up at St. Paul's Cathedral, but we gawk anyway. Then I feel a tug on my hand, and my daughter points towards a door on the side of the building. Lowering my gaze, I see what she sees. . .a woman sitting on the pavement, her dark blue skirt covering her legs. A gauzy black veil drapes down on either side of her time-worn face like a theater's curtains left half open. "Mommy, can I?" asks my daughter, holding up the bag of juicy purple grapes we'd purchased earlier from a street market. I nod and let her take the few remaining steps between us and the woman by herself. As I watch her squat down beside the woman and hold out her offering, my throat aches with a tenderness I cannot put into words.

naked stem. . .
an eternal gift
of grace

PART III | THE FORGOTTEN

THE COURT OF CATS

A gap-toothed smile stretched across
a roadmap of many lives lived out loud
in a single face

watery eyes the color of faded denim
or a tattered baby blanket, remnant of
a boy long grown

body stooped so low to the ground
that her skirt sweeps up discarded
candy wrappers,

cigarette butts, a neon-pink ball a kid
got from a quarter machine and lost
on the first bounce;

faltering steps lead her to a park bench,
warped on one end, green paint peeling
from sun and human sweat;

the pop of a tin tab breaks the silence;
a lean speckled tabby appears at her feet
as though summoned by the gods

then a black cat with half an ear gone,
a pin-striped gray, limping heroically, one
as yellow as the moon—and blind. . .

The Human Side

there is a sea of legs and fur and swishing
tails—plaintive howls from those with bellies
scraped bare like bowls

and she sits there upon her throne, crown
of gray, popping tab after tab, grateful subjects
winding between her legs.

PART III | *THE FORGOTTEN*

EVERY DAY IS AMBER

golden prism
        prison

                baked concrete
towers reflecting the sun

digging for coins
            under car seats

never enough

busting ass
            on the night shift

for a moldy studio
with broken A/C

generational poverty
            preserved.

The Human Side

HE HAD A NAME

I'd never seen a body before,
not a dead one,

but there he was, laid out like
a charcuterie board,

police tape blocking
the subway entrance.

"Poor Henry," I heard someone murmur;
"what a shame!"

I blinked back tears, hot with recognition
and regret.

Henry. A man I passed every day
on my way to work,

a gray, shrunken, stubbly figure
who used newspapers

the same way I use bedsheets;
I didn't see him—

not really, not even when I dropped an
occasional coin.

PART III | THE FORGOTTEN

He was camouflaged:
part city sidewalk,

part trashcan,
part grate.

Until he was dead.
Until I couldn't
ask. I never knew
he had a name.

The Human Side

THE LAST OF THEIR KIND

He was there on D-Day,
the sand from a beach
in Normandy
clinging to the bottom
of his boots.
He cannot forget
the smell of blood
or the screams
as men lay dying.
Over 4,400 never came home.

He was there
on April 11, 1945,
watching naked skeletons
reach for loaves of bread
in Buchenwald,
hot tears streaming
down his face.
Oh, the suffering,
how it haunted him,
still haunts him today.

She was there,
right under German noses,
sending codes they'd never break.
Tap, tap went her fingers
in the ghastly game
of cat and mouse.

If she were caught,
she'd hope for death—
for her lips were sealed
with secrets.

He was there
when Pearl Harbor
went down in flames,
sinking beneath
shells and torpedoes.
His lungs nearly burst
as he swam away
from the U.S.S. Arizona
his skin on fire
in the oil-slicked waves.

She was there
during the night raids
in London,
picking pieces of people
out of the rubble
stitching on arms and legs
if they could be saved.
Up to her elbows in guts,
living on soup
and three hours of sleep.

Less than 500,000 are left,
out of the 16 million Americans
who served.
And when we lay
the last one in the ground,

The Human Side

    beneath the colors
    for which they fought,
    we can bow our heads and say:
    there goes the last of their kind.

PART III | *THE FORGOTTEN*

LEFT BEHIND

brick walls,
auto locks,
prison for those
whose only crime
was getting old—

restless hands
clutch edges
of worn blankets
and memories
in hollow laps;

minutes tick,
monotony squeaks
on linoleum floors,
loose gowns
drape bony frames;

watery eyes stare,
blank slates,
brains like Swiss cheese;
time slips through
the holes.

THE HUMAN SIDE

LONELINESS

You stand
with your hands pressed
against the sides of the glass.

You're not sure when you dropped
into that long-necked bottle—
or who put the cork in the top.

You gaze out at the world—
a kaleidoscope of colors and people,
moving, swirling—a mosaic of busyness.

So, this is what people do—
shop, eat, laugh, argue, hold hands,
scold small children, sit at traffic lights.

But you, here in the bottle,
you do nothing but watch.
No one hears your muffled cries;
no one sees your breath fogging the glass
or sees tears pooling at your feet.

You draw a happy face
in the foggy mist,
and you shoulder-shove against the bottle,
heaving it on its side.

PART III | THE FORGOTTEN

The bottle tumbles and rolls,
through the streets,
kicked by restless feet,
over a curb, down a hill, into the sand.

It comes to rest—at last
where land meets sea.
You nudge the bottle
toward the hypnotic waves
then cast yourself, bottle and all,
into the endless froth of white and blue.

Someone will find me, you think.
I'm a message in a bottle;
someone will open the cork
and see what's inside.

The Human Side

MISS GERTIE NEXT DOOR

My neighbor often knelt before organized oases
of flowers: asters, bee balm, daisies, lamb's ear
—and mowed like a man, wearing overalls and
a floppy straw hat, probably because she had no

husband—but she could also crochet lace doilies
and make puffy quilted rag dolls with tiny button
eyes, clear signs of practiced domestication.
She left fresh bouquets on people's front porches

and sometimes a plate of sugar cookies covered in
plastic wrap, but she wasn't one for conversation
or poking her head through her blinds every time
a kid made a ruckus in the street. She minded her

own, and wore round sunglasses at the supermarket.
I once asked my mom why Gertie work dark glasses
inside the store, but Mom said that was *Miss Gertie*
to me, and I should hush my mouth. Then she got a

faraway look in her eyes and muttered something
about when a husband hires a cute, long-legged
filly as his secretary, it's not uncommon to put his
old mare out to pasture. I didn't know much about

horses, but I put an apple in Miss Gertie's mailbox
all the same.

PART III | THE FORGOTTEN

THE NATURE OF ONE

As I drive through a winding path in a national park, I see a lone female goat on top of a ridge. And when I say lone, I mean there isn't another animal anywhere near her in that golden stretch of nothingness. And I have to wonder, aloud to myself, for there is no one else in the car, whether she has a mate. Do goats mate for life? I don't know. Perhaps she once had a mate—but that mate wandered off because of her passion for mayonnaise instead of mustard, because she sipped red wine while he guzzled beer, or because he had a mid-life crisis and took a fancy to white fur instead of brown. Hard to say, really. So, I salute the goat and keep driving, hoping to see a bear.

wind-blow hair
lonely cheeks
have tears

The Human Side

NO PLACE TO CALL HOME

Loose papers flutter
down Market Street,
a man holds a sign:
Need somethin' to eat.
He's just one of many,
tattered hat, no shoes
nowhere to go,
and nothing to lose.

The ol' Golden State
don't shine for some,
most just livin'
on a prayer and a crumb.
Got dirt on their faces,
newspapers for bed,
a bottle for comfort;
one day they be dead.

Ain't no Hollywood
in these parts, my son
you live by your wits
and sleep with a gun.
Cracked-tooth smiles
beggin' pennies each day,
damned if they go;
damned if they stay.

PART III | THE FORGOTTEN

He's got a needle
and a dragon tattoo;
he got no idea,
he made local news.
One of 8,000
don't matter to him;
give him a burger;
give him some gin.

He's just one of many,
tattered hat, no shoes,
nowhere to go,
and nothing to lose.

SHALLOWS

Hollow, scraped bare; they
totter on the edge
      of humanity,
feet cut to shreds by shells
in the sand, but not daring
      to breach the deep.
Many once rode the waves,
before life wrestled them
      to the ocean floor.
Now the shallows disperse
them to bus stations and
      benches in the park,
where they become food
for the crabs, along with
      plankton and worms,
invisible to those who wear
rose-colored glasses and sip
      champagne on ice.

SHUT INS

Flash back to church services:
pray for the elderly and shut-ins,
such a routine request
as if elderly and shut-ins
are on the same list as
buy toilet paper at the market;

now here I sit—shut in. Bum leg,
staring at crosswords with no answers
waiting for the doorbell;
doorbells don't ring much,
no one presses them anymore.

I press my face against the glass,
like a child, leaving my nose print;
who is not shut in?
who gets to walk a dog?
who gets to vacation in Mexico?

Pray for the elderly and shut-ins;
wish now I'd done a little more than pray;
the elderly and shut-ins can't see prayers.
should have rung some doorbells,
should have pressed a prayer

on someone's forehead.

The Human Side

THINGS WE DON'T MENTION

She throws her head back
and laughs at her own joke,

and everyone else laughs too; they
can't help themselves.

She would juggle bowling pins
and perform clever card tricks

to keep people entertained if she could pull it off...

because as long as the people around
her are transfixed

by her effervescent trifles,
they will never know

about her solitary sobs in the dark or
that she
        hates
                her face
in the mirror

or that she can't drag herself out of bed some
days, even on the brightest mornings.

She's told no one of her *condition,*
as none would understand,

and a few might even say she's silly and tell her
she must *snap out of this funk.*

She knows because she tried, once, to hint
at the chaos entombed behind her eyes

during a late-night confessional
to one of her closest friends,

but the friend didn't understand how someone
so *beautiful and successful* could ever feel
badly about herself, and had even said, "I'll
gladly trade you places!"

But no. No, she wouldn't—not if she
knew about the corybantic dreams,

not if she could see the ridges on
her wrist from where she'd tried

        to release the anguish
                that raked her insides
into compost.

So, she will model picturesque smiles and
squeal with feigned delight

over so-n-so's engagement and
another's bedding selection for a crib

The Human Side

as she sips red wine on the balcony
and adjusts the stack of silver bangles

on her arm.

PART III | THE FORGOTTEN

THROUGH THE LENS

Based on the life of Polish photographer Wilhelm Brasse

Their eyes are as still as pond water—
that is to say, they don't move at all,
left wide open—as if surprised by their fate,
and yet I know they had feared this moment daily,
a fear worse than death.

Grown men, women and children alike—
skeletal waifs in tattered prison pajamas,
long ago stripped of their shoes and dignity,
left with not even their names to make them human;
my name is 3444.

My hands shake as I adjust the lens;
a new prisoner, now framed, stares defiantly.
Oh, how I wish her rage could sustain her,
but in days she will be but a shadow of her former self,
cowered by the ashes of Auschwitz.

Never, in all my years of training,
did I imagine I would photograph apocalyptic evil.
Oh, if my aunt could see me now...
Wilhelm, she would whisper—how can this happen?
I hang my head, ashamed.

Not that I was given a choice—
or at least not a choice I was willing to make,

The Human Side

that of pledging allegiance to a monster
and condoning the annihilation of these innocents,
guilty only as Jews.

And so, I was captured and assigned;
this is the cross I bear upon my shoulders,
and from this lens I must watch unspeakable horrors,
bruises, blood and broken bones—experiments gone awry...
click, click, click.

I swear when all of this is over,
if I make it out with sound body and mind,
I will never again press the shutter of a camera,
for I will not be able to bear the cold-sweat nightmares
of all my eyes have seen.

PART III | THE FORGOTTEN

VAGRANT

jagged edges—raw, red
fingernails chewed
to the quick

are you stupid? That's the
ten-dollar question
everyone asks

hidden in clothes two sizes
too big—all black
not blending,

a foreigner without a map;
no one gave you
the secret code

to life, not the mom with
greasy hair and
glazed green eyes,

not the dad whom you've
never met; you're
a canoe—cut

from its moorings, adrift
in unchartered
waters; paddles

The Human Side

absent—gone overboard;
raised eyebrows
slap the sides—

waves of disappointment,
or worse, pity
wash over the bow,

drowning, air sucked from lungs
the cuts on your arms
spell out *save me*.

PART III | THE FORGOTTEN

WRITE FOR ME

It was in the golf club smoking lounge (where no smoking is allowed) that I overhead a conversation between two literary elites.

I was trying to mind my own, with a roll of paper towels under one arm and glass cleaner in my other hand, but it was hard to ignore the cerebral electricity.

I have such a penchant, said one man, *for the exploration of the existential being.* I kept wiping tabletops, but nearly split my face with a grin.

Ah! Yes! said the other. *I did come across one piece the other day I found particularly intriguing. I've got the copy here. Shall I read it aloud?*

Oh, please do! I said in my head.

The man cleared his throat and began: *Vagrant waste stretched taut with fury silence in the stills—evening: wafer thin razors over bars that bind the rats.*

The Human Side

I waited, but that was it.

Profound, said the first man. *I can feel it here.* He points to the center of his chest. I'm not sure if he means his heart or a bad case of acid reflux.

I move on to the mantle, bringing my feather duster with me. The reading man mentions another piece, something about goats and windchimes—

but I'm no longer listening. I'm thinking if I was an editor, I'd be looking for poems that actually speak to people like me. Or, if I was a writer, I'd write something like this:

black and white—the color of my uniform,
the color of my duties,
the color of my life

no one asks me what colors I like; it
doesn't matter as long as I do my job and
don't complain

my stockings are too tight and my legs ache
with the weight of my body and the world on
my shoulders

PART III | THE FORGOTTEN

*I carry me; I carry my daughter, the one
whose father disappeared in the night six
years ago*

*speak English, they say, and I do, except
when I'm alone at night and I call out
Dios me salve—God save me.*

The men leave the smoking room
(where no one can smoke) and I
pick up their empty cups, their
candy wrappers, and the copy of the
poem for which the one man had
such a *penchant*—and throw them
all in the trash.

PART IV

The Grieved

ANCIENT STORIES

Oh, how I wanted to touch her, but I didn't dare—not with the signs and the park rangers and the threat of imprisonment and fines. So, I squatted on the beach, a safe and legal distance away, blubbering like a toddler in the throes of a tantrum because I wanted to hear her stories; I wanted to hear her tales of creation and the rise and fall of man, about her journey beneath the bowels of Noah's ark and how she'd added her salty tears to the sea when Jesus died on the cross. I wanted to place my hand on that dark, water-weathered shell and ask her what I should do with my life, post-menopause, post children. Surely, she would know—surely, she had seen my kind before, clutching sand and hope in the palms of her hands.

seaweed floats
wisdom slips
into the water

The Human Side

"ATLAS SHRUGGED"

Title from Ayn Rand's novel, 1957

The great Titan once held
the world on his shoulders—

brawny beams taut with
muscles that bulged under

the weight—I'm not sure why
Atlas passed *me* the globe

with its hues of brown, green
and blue, but he literally raised

his hands and lifted his burden
as though it were nothing but a

gumball from a vending machine.
You can imagine my surprise when

I stumbled under its unexpected
weight—when I felt the mountains

pressing against my collar bones—
when oceans ran down my cheeks,

when deserts and loamy earth sifted
onto my lashes. I blinked and blinked,

but I could never see as clearly again.
Why—I asked the Greek. *Why have you*

given me the world; me as thin as a
sapling? Atlas just looked at me

and shrugged.

The Human Side

BEHIND THE SMILE

lies a cavern of lies,
scars of past wounds
no one knew,
not when you smiled
and said you were fine,
not when you averted
your eyes
and swallowed hard
to keep tears at bay;
no one has time
for the truth anyway;
it's awkward to speak
of the secrets we keep,
memories of choices,
voices filling your ears
as you sleep. They say
you are strong, and you
long to be as strong as
they think, like you're
not on the brink of a cliff
getting ready to fall, so
you stand tall and face
strangers as if there's
no danger of losing your
mind and tell yourself
you were never designed
to break.

PART IV | THE GRIEVED

CATACOMBS

Cool fingers of air lift the
hairs on my neck

as my nose inhales the earthy scent
of ancient soil faithfully carved with drops of
saintly sweat centuries before my birth.

Descending into sunken chambers, as if I am
sleepwalking to my own burial, the flickering
yellow torch of rusted oil lamps pulls me into
slanted ghoulish shadows.

Sarcophagi perch, like sun-bleached bones, in
the recesses of each wall—hidden from all but
those who dare to embrace the ghost of San
Sebastian.

I count myself among the bravest of souls
beneath that hollowed, hallowed ground
until I turn the corner and see. . .

there, in a waning bobble of light, barely
longer than a shoe box, sits an exquisite
sarcophagus graced with an effigy of a child
just born.

Stillborn.

The Human Side

Etched deep into the stone, the face of his
anguished mother extends an intimate tether
to *all* mothers who have clutched a tiny
body that was never meant to breathe.

Shadows and light smear together, and I
clamp my hands over my mouth to keep
the paralyzing pain buried in the
catacombs of my heart,

where the soil still showcases
the imprints of my fists. . .

and not a drop of saintly
sweat.

PART IV | THE GRIEVED

HARMONIOUS CACOPHONY

All day I hear the frenetic beeping of taxi horns, the staccato rat-tat-tat of shoes upon the pretentiously polished floors of Draco, Miles, Smith, & Ellis LLP., phones ringing, papers shuffling from within the solitary confines of the *aesthetic* blue cubicles, the ping of e-mails piling atop the 48 unread e-mails from yesterday. A friend of mine, who lives outside the city, asked me the other day when she visited the office, "How can you even think with all this noise?" That's the problem, though, I *can* think—clearly! I guess I have a waffle brain that plops each sound into separate compartments like dollops of syrup, which allows an excruciating amount of time to think about the three words that changed my life last month: you've—got—cancer. In that moment, I felt like I'd been tackled by a middle linebacker; the air whooshed out of my lungs. My non-city friend begged me to *get outside* more often, so I've been taking her advice. I could hole up somewhere quiet, I suppose, but I've chosen to take the ferry across the bay where the seagulls scream and screech with reckless abandon. I imagine it's hunger that drives them to act so raucously, but it doesn't matter. I revel in the brashness

The Human Side

of their voices, and sometimes I scream too, as loudly as I can, and my voice blends seamlessly with theirs as they dip and dive about my ears. From this side of the water, the city looks like a miniature movie set, where people might have cancer. And I'm nothing more than a dark body with a thousand wings.

PART IV | THE GRIEVED

THE HOLLOW

One drop of blood. Only one. No need to panic. But I panic; hyperventilate. An hour later, I'm looking into the grim face of an ultrasound technician. Cool gel squishes across my extended belly, and I listen, desperate for the steady sound: whump, whump, whump. "Let me go get the doctor," she says. Hot tears squeeze out of my eyes and run down the sides of my face, dribbling into my ears. *No!* I scream inside my head. "Let's take a look," the doctor says (too brightly) as he enters the room. More gel lands on my belly in a blob. Squish, squish. Silence. Dear God, the silence. "I'm afraid he's gone," the doctor says. "I'm so sorry." *No!* This time my scream is audible.

a cracked egg
mother picks aimlessly
at sticks in her nest

INTERLUDE

Down,
          down,

I descend
into the Paris underground.

      Faces blur
like a watercolor painting; voices hum;

      too many bees in the hive.
I feel most alone in a crowd;

      don't belong—where is home?
Then—a keening cry rises,

      like smoke from a bonfire
bow against string, mating—

      lover on lover, violin
dripping notes in D minor,

      my nose dripping snot,
face charcoaled with mascara,

      tears traveling like trains
on parallel tracks—no brakes.

      I don't care if it's Bach

PART IV | THE GRIEVED

or Beethoven; I open my soul

    to catch symphonies
like a child catches rain

    on her tongue.

The Human Side

JUST FOR THE NIGHT

like a paper bag left too long in the rain,
your face shreds into waterlogged pieces;

not that it was firm in the REM recesses
of my mind, but rather like a fog of breath

in winter air—suspended between fluttering
eyelids and that first knife of sunlight cutting

through blinds. And so, I remain, caught like a
fly in the complex web between wake and sleep,

my fingers fumbling for purchase on the jagged
rocks of my dream—if I can hold on longer,

you might turn from gas to solid; you might
pull on faded jeans with a hole in the pocket;

you might tuck the worn quilt under my chin,
and tell me it's your turn to make breakfast.

A LIFETIME OF ELLIPSES

that associate degree
you left hanging
like a bedsheet on the clothesline,

unfinished artwork,
canvases covered
in dust-smudged birds without wings.

You were going to be
an EMT, but you got
a pedicure and went to beauty school.

Backpacked across Europe,
came home disillusioned,
decided to work in an auto parts store.

If only I could still your restless feet,
hand you contentment
the way one hands out chocolate bars.

But as long as you continue
to run with three dots trailing behind you,
no one, not even me, can place a period

THE HUMAN SIDE

REVELATION: YOUR MOM HAS A BRAIN TUMOR

Nothing made sense—Mom suddenly
couldn't walk. She was walking fine

one day then the next day, her legs
wouldn't move. The doctors didn't

know anything; so, they pulled rabbits
out of hats like white-caped magicians:

tests...physical therapy...pills...socks...

Nothing. As her motor skills diminished,
like water swirling round and round,

down the drain,

the brick building marked her—one side
for getting-better patients, the other side,

you ain't leaving. She got moved to 106.

Hair. Unbrushed. Carrots. Dropped.

Finally, one doctor had an epiphany—MRI.
Months of unanswered questions appeared

on a blurry black and white film.

What's that saying? A day late and a dollar
short? So, we held her hands and matched

her shallow breaths until the angels
gave her wings.

The Human Side

ROWS NOT PLANTED

Cows graze in the meadow. . .crisp, green salads in abundance after the April rains. The scene might suggest serenity were it not for the young woman in the cowboy hat and green-flannel shirt kicking at a fresh mound of six-foot-long dirt. "You said forever!" she shouts at muted ground. But she knows, even as she rages, that the preacher had added the caveat. . .'till death do you part." She had idealistically assumed that the preacher meant the newlyweds would grow old together and one day play with their grandchildren while rocking on the front porch— complaining about arthritis. He never once mentioned, during all of the "I do's" that the neighbors would soon huddle in secluded groups to whisper about the *tractor accident*, sighing and shaking their heads while acknowledging that *these things happen.*

a lone wolf howls—
as the sun dips
below the horizon

PART IV | *THE GRIEVED*

SELLING GRIEF

a staccato beat

Who will give me $100, $100, $100—
do I hear $100?

Sold.

A widow sells her grief
piece-by-piece.

THE HUMAN SIDE

TABLE FOR ONE

6 a.m. Lunches are packed. Two pieces of toast sit on the counter with pools of thick yellow butter slowly melting across their surfaces. I take a bite out of one and go rouse my daughter, Emma. "Wake up sleepy head. Our busses will be coming soon." She yawns dramatically and begins her auto-pilot routine of dressing and brushing her hair. Then comes the flurry of backpacks, socks, shoes, and coats—and me, trying to find my work apron. Once outside, I kiss my 9-year-old on the head. "Love you," I say. "Love you more," she says. Her breath comes out in little cold puffs then she turns and waves (backwards) as she walks in the opposite direction to her bus stop.

As I sit looking out of the window of my bus, which will take me to the Crack of Dawn Café, I wonder if Emma will have any childhood scars from the life I've given her. Every day we scurry through our routines, me to work, her to school—then her to homework and me to school. She once asked me, about three years ago, why she didn't have a dad. I told her that her dad was like having a mega case of heartburn for two months and after that, he'd simply disappeared, taking all of the antacids with him. I'm sure she'll ask more questions someday, but that's been enough of an explanation so far.

a solitary light
darkness dispersing
into corners

PART IV | THE GRIEVED

TALKING TO GOD

If I were to bang on the door
throw myself on the floor
ask God *why* while I cry
in frustration and pain, nothing
to lose, nothing to gain,
just raw rage at the life, made
worse by a curse that drapes
over my frame like weight,
weighing insane; should I sit
in sackcloth and ash—this won't
last says my friends who mean well
but tell me nothing to bring me out
of this pit; I don't fit, don't belong,
just square pegs in round holes—
God, are you listening?

God knocks at my door, throws
Himself on my floor, puts His face
next to mine; I'm blind with His light;
His white robe flows—He speaks;
I listen like Job: Were you *there*
when I formed the sea? Do you hold
the key to Heaven or Hell? Can you tell
me when I made the sun, spun stars in
the sky, gave birds wings to fly, gave
birth to the earth, imprinted the land
with My feet in the sand? Were you
there when I formed you in the depths

The Human Side

of the womb? You're not in a tomb.
Do not despair, I made the atoms and
air that you breathe, I am *He*. I Am.

PART IV | THE GRIEVED

TRANSIENT

I'll burrow beneath goose-down covers. Soon you'll turn; we'll spoon. I love the predictability of our shapes. Then, as the sun is dripping its buttery light into the blue-black morning, we'll have coffee and eggs (yours over-easy), and we'll watch the news—you, grumping about those vapid politicians who talk out of both sides of their mouths. With a hand on one hip and that ornery, cock-eyed grin, you'll say: *I've already forgotten more than they'll ever know!* I will laugh, and we'll take synchronized sips from our mugs. But I know, in spite of the going-to-hell-in-a-handbasket predictions you always make about our world, you'll put on your green flannel shirt, those forever-grease-stained mechanic jeans, and beat-up brown boots—and go to work. Because that's who you are.

Who you were.

quiet kitchen
uneaten oatmeal in
the sink

THE HUMAN SIDE

TWO PEAS IN DIFFERENT PODS

She was the older sibling, her
brother—the younger.

She was religion, he was
hidden magazines.

Her brother was a failed pancreas
absent of insulin; she was *worry* in
front of God's gate.

He was leaving with the divorce;
She was sweeping up pieces of glass
and heart.

Her brother was walking a razor's edge
rolling joints; she was picking threads of lies
from his eyes.

He was dead a couple of times, paddled back to life,
she was counting money in a cash register, eating
cereal for dinner.

She wanted to find him.

Her brother was disappearing into the smoke of
cigarettes, drowning in black coffee; she was
saving Christmas presents in the closet.

PART IV | *THE GRIEVED*

He wore rebellion like a coat; she beat
the odds with her brain.

She's the girl with salt on her pillowcase.

WASTING DISEASE

I watched my fish grow
thinner and thinner.

Someone told me they had
wasting disease.

                      I had that too after
the   ghost

of you plagued my nights with
what ifs

Someone said they could see
my clavicle.

Who says stuff like that?

But it was true.

                My clavicle

nearly broke in two.

PART IV | *THE GRIEVED*

WEAR YOUR BEST BLACK

"She looks so at peace," they say. "Like she passed away in her sleep," they say. And I want to scream. Why do people talk about the dead that way? My grandma didn't even look like that when she slept—arms all folded over her chest like some damn vampire in a box. My grandma slept with one leg sticking out of the covers, arms akimbo, her springy gray curls mushed up on one side of her head. I smile now, in spite of the heat spreading across my cheeks. I need to escape this gauche display which has been lauded "a celebration of Maureen's life." Oh, I know they will want to prattle on about her homemade blackberry jam, *best in the county*, and mention that time the mule got out and that Maureen, *God love her heart chased that fool animal down and drove it back to its pen with a spatula.* They will want to brag about her fair queen days—*prettiest little thing you ever did see.* But I won't listen; my feet will carry me back across the field of harvest-ready corn, back into our farmhouse (which is older than Grandma was), and into her bedroom on the first floor. I will lie in her bed, snuggled under her ragged patchwork quilt— the quilt that once belonged to her grandma—and I will not remember the way she looked today. I will remember the way she put red licorice under my pillow while I was at school, and the way she warmed up my coat on top of the old stove before I went out to catch the bus, and the way we giggled together in my fort under the apple tree. The wind whisks briskly through the partially open window, and I feel Grandma's hand brush my bangs out of my eyes.

casseroles grow cold—
faded Gladiolus
poke out of the trash

The Human Side

WHEN MY BRAIN WAS A BUCKET

Intelligent, sharp, quick-witted—those
were all adjectives used to describe me
before

then my brain stepped in gum, or
the equivalent thereof,
at least that's what the doctors say;

they use fancier words, of course,
degeneration, dementia, neurons— all
that to compare my brain to a sieve.

I should be insulted; some days I am, and
I recite poetry, crochet, and invent new
recipes to prove I can still hold water.

PART IV | THE GRIEVED

WHERE THE LOST THINGS GO

My only daughter holds my hand;
I know who she is today, and I
squeeze my eyes shut, trying to
lock in the memories. She's
speaking—softly. "Do you
remember, Mom,
when I was just a little girl—and I
would always lose a mitten, just one
mitten? And you would ask me:
'Where, darling, is your other mitten?'
I never knew.
My answer would always be:
'It must have gone where the lost things go.'"

I laugh softly. I do remember. I do.
Holding one mitten in my hand,
asking my Isabel that question. I can
almost smell the cold, can almost see Isabel's tiny pink nose.
Oh, how that girl would lose things!
Socks!
"You would do the same with socks." I say.
She pats my hand and nods.
"Yes," she says, "How could I lose just
one?" I shrug. "You didn't mind so much. . .
you loved mismatches anyway."
Isabel smiles. "I just figured the other socks
must have gone where the lost things go."

The Human Side

"Well," I say, putting my other hand on top of hers, "At least you never lost your children."
Isabel giggles, still that little-girl giggle from long ago. "You're right, Mom. I never lost my girls. Although they loved to hide in your old apple tree!" I nod, as flashes of red headed curls and toothless grins sweep before my eyes.
"Do they lose stuff?" I ask her.
"They used to," she answers. "But now that they are older, they mostly find where the lost things go."
I nod. Something is slipping, and I place one hand on my head, trying to hold on. Hold on. Maybe today I won't...Some nice lady is patting my hand, a pretty red head with lots of curls.
I like this one.
"It's OK, Mom," she whispers.
Mom...what does she mean?
"Who am I?" I ask.
Maybe I remind her of someone.
No matter. She rubs my cheek as a little tear runs down her own. "I know you're in there," she says, "I know you're where the lost things go.

WHIFFLER

Suffocating, bodies pressing on
every side, the clack and squeak of
a thousand pairs of shoes on waxed
tile floors...

I could not travel without my
whiffler, the one who walks in
front of me in a crowd, the one
wearing a red flannel shirt and
sturdy brown boots and that
ridiculous oversized fisherman's
hat.

I used to be able to go it
alone, before the
breakdown, before the past
reattached itself
to my back
like cat claws
in a knit sweater...

now I keep my eyes glued
on the broad body who
deftly parts the waters, like
God parted the Red Sea
for Moses and the Israelites,

The Human Side

and I, too, walk on dry ground
with the aqua walls suspended on
either side;
Pharaoh cannot touch me.

I see the Promised Land.

PART V

The Resilient

PART V | THE RESILIENT

BEYOND GETTING EVEN

The more he rages,
the more she tucks
inside herself—
arms, legs, shoulders,
under the piano bench—
like a child who thinks
if she can't see
then she can't be seen.

She's *not* a child,
just barely,
having said *I do*
at age 18.
But she's unfamiliar
with broken lamps,
splintered doors
and car windows that
shatter
into her lap
before she drives away.

"Why do you let him?"
her sister asks.
"You used to have
so much sass!
Now you're a mouse
sitting in a corner."
Her sister is not wrong.

The Human Side

She feels whiskers
growing,
as she timidly nibbles the
cheese.

But that one question
niggles at the back of her
brain.
It's there when she fights
against his weight,
knuckles held to the floor.
It's there when her back
hits the chair
and sports a baseball size
bruise.
The question won't let her
go!
She wrestles it while giving
the dog a bath—
bakes it in the oven with a
casserole—
takes it to church on Sunday—
dusts it off every shelf—
sweats through it in her
dreams—
takes it to the courthouse—
then has it mailed
to him.

She shaves off the whiskers
and throws out the cheese,
(now that she has the answer)

then celebrates herself with
not one degree
but three.

THE HUMAN SIDE

CLOSE THE DOOR ON YOUR WAY OUT

can't say I'm sorry to see you go;
it's been a long time coming—this parting
of ways

we were never in sync anyway,
at opposite ends of every spectrum—so,
you're fired;

clear out that cubicle you jackknifed
into my life, the one you overstuffed with
narcissism;

take your emotional manipulation;
it's probably next to your stapler and
scissors;

don't leave pity pictures on the wall;
I won't need reminders of your manic
shenanigans;

turn around, and don't look back;
I'm propping up my bare feet,
finding Zen;

close the door on your way out.

CONQUERING MOUNTAINS

The road might take a sharp turn;
dreams will be crushed at your feet,
like cigarette butts in a gutter,
all you will see is defeat.

But, girl, hold your head up,
Rocky fists raised high in the air,
If someone says, "You can't do this,"
You say, "Is that a dare?"

Fight as long as you have to;
pull your boots up by their straps;
if you ever feel like you're lost,
don't forget *you* have the maps.

Just because no one has done it,
does not mean it cannot be done;
you just gotta stay grounded,
even when you're dying to run.

Education never comes easy,
whether in books or in life;
be fearless when facing your failures,
even when they cut like a knife.

The Human Side

Some mountains will be imposing;
your hands might slip when you climb,
but when you put your flag at the top,
you can say, "This mountain is mine!"

*For Nicole

EULOGY TO MY FORMER SELF

The fence at last stands taut and tall,
a boundary firmly placed.
She learned the art of saying no
with a smile upon her face.
She no longer walks on eggshells,
to shield your fragility;
she burnt that prison to the ground
and threw away the key.
As she cut the ropes that bound her
and took her final breath,
she knew she'd found the secret;
there's organic life in death.

The Human Side

EXCUSE ME

while I sit in a chair
like a rain-soaked leaf
like a beached jelly fish
missing a vertebrae.

Excuse me
while I take a shower
stand five minutes too long
stand like a sunburnt palm
dripping exhaustion.

Excuse me
while I refuse to adult
break down for a second
break like a dam
crying my eyes out.

Excuse me
while I tune out kids
like a soundproof room
like expensive headphones
cradling silence.

Excuse me
while I eat a sandwich
like I'm five years old
like it's the cat's meow
bologna and mustard.

PART V | THE RESILIENT

Excuse me
while I brush my teeth,
while I turn off the lights,
while I pad upstairs,
and sleep like winter.

THE HUMAN SIDE

FAILURE TO FAIL

Bet'cha thought you'd bought a front-row ticket
to the film of my epic failure,

and so, there you were,
feet propped up on the bar
in front of you, munching on
popcorn, sippin' your soda.

You were waiting for the good part—
the scene where I fall on my face
then beg you (faux noble one)
to help me up.

Oh, but you weren't counting
on the plot twist, were ya?
Never even saw it coming—me,
turning into Wonder Woman.

You literally stopped in mid chew,
I think—when I started burning down
Defeat
then stood triumphantly in the flames,
staring back at you.

Didn't know what to think, did ya,
when I walked across that stage
with a 3.96 and never looked back.

PART V | THE RESILIENT

You'll never do it without me,
those were the barbs you once
tossed over your back in the wake
of your pompous exit,

and yet. . .here I am, three degrees later,
watching you slink out of the theater,
your soda spillin' sideways on the floor.

FLIGHT

You kicked me out of the nest,
    thought I would spiral
    to my death

then looked taken aback
    when I didn't break my neck
    when I didn't get swallowed
    by the cat;

my wings caught the wind
    and I rode it like a stallion breaker—
    broke you, didn't I?
    made you cry

with fury because I was free
    no longer dependent on your worms,
    regurgitated
    leftovers.

PART V | THE RESILIENT

FRIEND REQUEST

It's not the first time
you've friend requested me,
but still—I stop stirring
my chai tea latte and click—

not to add you, but to review
the reasons why I won't add you—
ever! And. . .there it is, the shiny,
full-color photo of you leaning

against your office desk, arms
folded across your chest, wearing
a custom-made suit, Italian leather
shoes, and Louis Vuitton watch.

How do I know? Because you've
always had million-dollar tastes—
even on minimum wage salaries,
even when our cupboards were

bare, and the kids had holes
in their jeans. I would say congrats
on all your fancies, except I know
you're in debt up to your eyeballs

and you'll take the loan to that red
sports car you love like a mistress

The Human Side

    to your grave. I smile to myself
    as I hit decline, take a sip of my chai,

    and enjoy the exquisite
           quiet
    of a house
    that is all mine.

PART V | THE RESILIENT

GIVE MY REGARDS

to the past,
ain't looking back,
I'm back in the game,
a real game-changer,
changing my decisions,
deciding to live for me,
life is too short for regrets,
regretting only that I stayed
too long in my stays, but
I broke free, freeing my mind
and soul, minding my own,
I got dreams, dreaming in
bold print, printing my feet,
making tracks. Track my progress;
give my regards to the past.

The Human Side

THE HUMAN STORY

Scars that have faded
to a ghostly white
delegated to the back
of one's mind,
scars that are still pink—
fresh with recent memories;
each of our arms
are marked in some way,
whether visible or not.

Don't we all have stories?
Those dark places
we keep beneath
the shiny exterior
of our white-toothed smiles,
and when asked,
"How are you"
in passing,
we all say, "Just fine."

And who's to say my story
is more traumatic than yours
or that yours
is more traumatic than mine?
Do we need to x-ray
each other's chests
to find out whose heart
has more bullet holes?

PART V | THE RESILIENT

Pasts riddled with
fathers who scream,
mothers who drink,
a boyfriend
who likes smashing faces
into concrete,
a child who died,
a body consumed by disease,
a leg blown off
in the land of sand and hate,
a mind that stopped remembering,
a mind that remembers too much.

So, put away the measuring sticks.
There are no blue ribbons;
we're all just participants
in the span of time
allotted to us.
Live with all of the grace
and dignity one can muster
for you're no more (or less)
human than I am;
I am no more (or less)
human than you.

The Human Side

I BELIEVE

I believe in hard work,
not handouts.
I believe in honesty
(even brutal).
I believe in action verbs
because passive
is weak and unproductive.
I believe in imagination;
there is a dash of
mermaid and dragon
in all of us.
I believe in love, just not
the Harlequin kind. Bare-
chested Finn—Pshaw!
I believe in rooting for
the underdog, regardless
of the odds.
I believe in principles
and holding the line,
but I also believe
in forgiveness.
I believe in lucky bamboo
even if it dies,
and I believe in flowers
that grow through cracks
in the sidewalk.
I believe in tenacious
dependability; after all,

if you are not as good as
your word, you are
worthless.
I believe in hope, that
Ancient Elixir passed
down by kings and peasants
alike—the remedy for all
that is dark and lost.

IN MY ALTERNATE LIFE

I stand in a Paris subway station running a bow across the strings of a violin—not because I need money but because the violin weeps music into the vast underground and makes people, who never stop for anything, grind to a halt.

In my alternate life

I am fluent in Spanish, Italian, German and French—in perfect cadence, syllables drop from my tongue as smoothly as melted butter. I say buenos dias, buon giorno, guten morgen, bonjour as breezily as I say good morning in my native tongue.

In my alternate life

I sweep a charcoal pencil across a blank sketch pad in the middle of Central Park. Lines and shadows become trees, bridge, bench—an old lady extending a hand, ripe as a withered apple, to the pigeons gathered like sentinels near her sandal-clad feet.

In my alternate life

I look out over a river from my office with a view, smiling at the grand stack of manuscripts on my desk. Today I will read, edit, fulfill the dreams of some, crush the dreams of others (in the nicest way)—eat roasted turkey on toasted sourdough bread with mayonnaise for lunch, saving crust for the geese when I walk home.

PART V | THE RESILIENT

INSIDE INGREDIENT

I guess I never really knew my mom until the day my dad drove away in a new red Ferrari and never returned. My mom had always been—pristine. Orderly. Some of my friends would say stiff. What I didn't know was that the rod in her back had been inserted by my dad. Just days before my high school graduation, I came home to find my mom up to her elbows in flour— with a defiant dab on her nose. "I'm a baker," she proclaimed, with the widest, most honest grin I'd ever seen. She'd made scones, baguettes, and crêpes. I swear she'd even developed a charming French accent. When she opened a bakery, I took a picture of her golden baguettes nestled in brown paper bags and framed it for my wall.

two cups of confidence
a pinch of resilience
mix well

THE HUMAN SIDE

LOOKING FOR THE SPIRIT

So, I was 'bout as dry as a sun-bleached
bone, and 'bout as white, too—when
someone told me to get myself down
to the West Side Baptist church
cause they got the Spirit down there
and treat people as fine as silk pajamas.
So I slipped into the back pew feeling
pretty conspicuous, as I was the only
white person there, but that choir
got to singing, and the notes hit the rafters
and bounced around like glass marbles
in a fishbowl, and pretty soon, I joined in,
swaying like a willow in a windstorm,
eyes closed, hands lifted to God. Then
the preacher got up there and revved up—
like one of those cars that do 0–60 in three seconds,
and all the people said "Amen, brother, Amen." And I
said, "Amen, brother, Amen." "Preach on," they said.
And I said, "preach on." And he did. He preached on
for little over an hour, and people started fanning.
Then came the calling,
"Who in here needs God today?" Clearly, I did,
so I went to the altar and they laid hands on me,
and I sure enough found the Spirit and started crying
so much I figured Jesus might have to walk on water
again. Then one of the ladies pressed a hanky in my
hand, which was 'bout the nicest thing anyone ever
gave me. They started clapping and singing "I'll Fly

Away." I sang too, and wings grew right out my back.
I flew around the rafters with them music notes
and didn't come down until somebody mentioned
there was fried chicken in the kitchen.

The Human Side

MOXIE

Compressed into a box,
the company's attempt
    at shape-shifting,

an elbow-shaped bump,
a knee that won't bend,
    gossip goes down like

burnt coffee, but she sticks,
like sweet gum burrs,
    endures side glances,

the buttoning of suits,
power posturing,
    the smell of money

and too much cologne—
no; she will not serve
    drinks or humble pie;

her chin was made for
pointing upward, an angle
    unmistakably sharp;

her sensible pumps clip
with purpose, like periods;
    her navy-blue jacket,

PART V | THE RESILIENT

well, that has buttons too;
and she can wield a pen
       like Joan of Arc

wielded a sword. There is
no real *war*, of course,
       just the undercurrent,

the age-old engagement
of patronizing patriarchy,
       versus a woman's moxie!

The Human Side

PURPLE HEARTS STILL BLEED

I was about 14 when I went into my dad's study and saw him holding a medal that lay in the center of a little velvet-lined box. "What's that?" I asked, and he looked up, slowly, but it didn't seem like he actually saw me. He was looking at a point beyond my shoulder. Finally, he said, "A purple heart." I looked at the heart, which held a gold bust of a man pressed against a cushion of purple. "What's it for?" I asked. He glanced back down at the medal. "It's...it's a...reward...for... bravery. I got it when I served in Nam." I knew my dad was prior military, but that had been before I was born, and we never talked about it. I'd seen his old uniform once, hanging in the back of the closet, and I'd asked him why he still had it, but he'd just shrugged and shut the closet door. "What did you do that was brave?" I asked, in a whisper. I'm not sure why, but it seemed right to speak softly. Dad's eyes glazed over, and he was silent for such a long time that I thought I should leave, but then he spoke: "My men were under fire.

We'd been ordered to pull out, but we were pinned down." I blinked as an image of wrestlers came to mind, but somehow, I didn't think that's what he meant. I stayed quiet. Dad suddenly put the box containing the medal on his desk and pulled his wallet out of his pocket. "Here," he said, showing a creased, faded-out picture. It looked old and was tinted light brown. "This is me," Dad said, pointing to a face in the middle of a group of about 20 men. It was odd to see my dad, shirtless, with a cigarette hanging out of his mouth, his arms around the two men closest to him. He had a grin on his face, but his eyes held a glint. *Bad ass* is what I thought, but I didn't say it aloud. "And this," Dad said, pointing, "is Billy Kemp, John Rogers, Phil Cobb, Jordan Banks, La'Shawn Font, George Sandford, Howie Lang, Jerome Watts, Tate Ford. . ." Dad's finger moved until he'd listed the name of every face in the photo—but one. "And this," his voice broke, "is Sunny Romero." Dad's mouth quirked up on one side. "Guys gave him hell about that name, so he eventually went by his nickname, D.J. because he was famous for playing vinyls on an old record player in the camp." Dad's voice softened then,

"The fool had that record player in his rucksack that day...not sure if he planned on spinning records during the...the fight, but..." Dad trailed off. My heart squeezed inside my chest as I saw unshed tears brimming in his eyes. I'd never seen my dad cry in my whole life. Dad shook his head as if to clear away the tears by sheer force. "Anyway," he said, coughing slightly into his hand. "I got shot in the leg, but I couldn't leave...I had to get my guys, you know? I was able to drag Phil and Howie out...but D.J....and the rest...the rest of the men..." Dad stood abruptly, opened his desk drawer and shoved the medal inside. He slammed the drawer with such force that I literally jumped back and gripped the edge of the door frame. I waited to see if he'd say anything else, but Dad seemed lost in his own world, one that I could never enter. That Christmas, I asked Dad if I could have a record player, and he gave me the strangest look. He got me one, though—and even helped me pick out some vintage vinyls from a second-hand store. I already had an eclectic range of music I listened to, so I was thrilled with his picks: Crosby Stills Nash & Young's *Dèjá Vu*, The Beatles' *Let it Be*, Van Morrison's *Moondance*, but my favorite was one that I found later, one that my dad had slipped into the pile without me noticing. I was going through the stack one day not long after Christmas and saw a post-it note stuck to the front of a Simon & Garfunkel album: *Bridge over Troubled Water*. The post-it simply read, "D.J.'s favorite" in my dad's scrawled handwriting. I bet I listened to that album five times a day. Dad never listened to any of the albums he got me, at least not in the same room, but at times I would see him standing in the doorway of his office. I knew he could hear, and I hoped his real heart was in a good place.

REINVENTION

Holding onto the frayed edges of a mistake I made when I was 18 years old, when I was hasty and headstrong and naïve to boot, I lie in bed, telling God I can't do this anymore. Yes, I know I took my vows before Him and man; yes, I know I said for better or worse—but did I say I would be willing to be stomped by arrogance, trampled with anger? Days pass. I can feel my palms dampen as I make that last curve around the sun and walk into the new year. This the time for resolutions. I climb the courthouse steps. When I come out, I feel weightless—floating on the helium high of my signature and the county stamp.

through a crack
in the sidewalk
a single flower

PART V | THE RESILIENT

THE SAYER OF GRACE

Fever. Cough. A positive test. He can't breathe. He sways when he stands. A daughter's call to the doctor. A doctor's call to the Emergency Room. He's on his way. Oxygen. Sweet, pure oxygen pumped into lungs besieged by crystals. I can hear his labored breaths over the phone. Keep talking, I say. I'm far away, but I'm with you in the sterile hospital room with its cool tile floors, white walls, and breezy-back gowns. I'm crying out to God. I will not let go of your hand—for five whole days, I will not let go. Ah—there you are. The release from the novel beast. Breathing on your own. You say the sunlight has refracted into a thousand tiny beams through your window shades. You say they will let you go home. You did it. You stubborn 84-year-old never-give-upper. What's that, Dad? You say you're hungry?

forks pause
over beef stroganoff
no atheists here today

SECOND SPRING

In the fall of her life
she refused to fade gray,
refused to wear flowered prints,
refused to let age brittle her bones.

In the fall of her life
she took painting classes,
took a fancy to champagne,
took no one and nothing for granted,
took a spin on the back of a motorcycle.

In the fall of her life
she traveled to Greece,
traveled to Philadelphia,
traveled to embrace the present,
traveled to unravel threads of the past.

In the fall of her life
she grew the greenest leaves,
grew a backbone made of steel
grew to love herself and her mistakes
grew seeds in the pockets of second spring.

PART V | THE RESILIENT

SHOESHINE IN TOKYO

An unassuming figure on bended knees,
shoulders hunched forward,
her eyes upon the feet of humanity,
swishes a clean, worn cloth back and forth.
An artist in her own right,
she creates a shiny canvas upon which
the soles of men may tread.

An unassuming figure encased by cardboard
and the steel-gray slabs of a buzzing Tokyo sidewalk
wears a simple flowered dress and egg-blue apron.
A queen in her own right,
she commands her polish to erase the stains
of the subway soot.

An unassuming figure with nimble black fingers,
surrounded by cans of Kiwi, cotton buffers,
and a cup of green tea,
makes no excuses or apologies for her career.
A business tycoon in her own right,
she tallies up her earnings in a leaf-brown binder
that's tied together with string.

A magician in her own right,
people remember *the lady who make shoes clean,*
and she
turns dirt
into Yen.

THE HUMAN SIDE

SQUEEZING THOSE LEMONS

You know that saying—
*when life gives you lemons
make lemonade?*
Well, I hate that saying,
and people be saying it to me
all the time!
Guess that's because I'm up
to my eyeballs in lemons—
and not because life gave them
to me, like somebody hand you
a present all tied up with a bow,
more like life be chucking them
at my head. Whack! Yep,
another lemon. Honestly! Those
folks who like to go around talking
in pretty phrases ain't got no idea
how much squeezing it takes to
get lemonade out of a lemon. I bet
they ain't even tried. But I did once,
just to see how long it take to get me
some lemonade out of yellow balls.
I got to lemon number thirty-two, and
had 'bout half a glass. So I figure I be
squeezing on lemons until the Lord
call me home. Might even take a few
up there with me—just in case.

PART V | THE RESILIENT

THINGS YOU CARRIED

Since time began, you carried the heartbeat
of all humanity,
knees, elbows, feet kicking in your belly,
new generations born.
You carried water pots upon your head,
your neck strong, unyielding.
Your bare feet made tracks in the dusty road,
sun hot on fierce bronze skin.
You carried skins and laid them in your lap,
sewn with animal bone.
You carried lullabies and remedies,
this—the root of the root...
You carried a secret nobody knows,
the rib from whence you came
contained the fearlessness and fortitude
of ten thousand brute men.
You carried woman in breasts, hips, and thighs,
world upon your shoulders.

The Human Side

WATERSHED MOMENT

when I deleted your number
from my contact list

when my eyes stayed bone dry
during your pity party

when I unplugged the cord
of your manipulation

when I slammed the door
on your whiskey breath

when I left you to fall in love
with your own reflection.

PART V | THE RESILIENT

"YOU ARE YOUR BEST THING"

Title from Toni Morrison's Beloved, 1987

Cast off arrowed words
dipped in poison;
meet haughty eyes
with warrior vibes.
You were born for this!

For this time
For this place
For this purpose

Crowns will tip
on heads hung down;
straighten it,
straighten up,
shoulders back.

Ah, they be too cool
for you? Reject those
lies, you got more fight
in your little finger
than all those fools.

Look in the mirror.
See your face, your braids
your grace—embrace it all.

THE HUMAN SIDE

Those eyes of gray and steel,
that iron will.

You are yours
You are best
You are your best thing.

For Makayla

PART V | *THE RESILIENT*

YOU'RE SITTING ON THE TRACKS

you feel the rumble of the engine
deep inside your chest,
rattling your ribcage;

you want to get up, but you can't;
it's like being in a dream—
everything in slow motion;

light blinds you, and you squeeze
your eyes shut to erase
the 200-ton horror;

the whistle slices both eardrums;
this is it, you think,
this is when I die,

but someone snatches you from
the tracks, neatly, warmly,
securely to her chest.

Her name is Hope.

THE HUMAN SIDE

YOU WANTED ME TO SPARE YOUR FEELINGS

but I spared your life instead
by telling you the truth
by getting to the root of the root
by making you face the looking glass
and the choices you made
when no one else was to blame
but you.
You can bury your soul in drink
but that won't bring you back
from the brink of the grave
where you buried a daughter.
You can't turn back the hands
of the clock nor can you block
the memories, but by God,
you can stop blaming me.

ZENITH

I stretch both arms high above my head,
my fists opening to the Maker of the stars.

My mistakes ride the wings of the wind,
like the cottony seeds of a dandelion.

Tears travel the worn path down my face,
but this time with water of redemption.

Amazing grace how sweet the sound;
My chains are gone; I've been set free.

Washed in forgiveness, I feel His presence;
it's in the fog of my breath that dispenses

into the cool night air; it's in the pine trees
to the East; it's in the Milky Way and moon.

My Zenith; my eternal hope; the One who
said, "Peace! Be still." And my soul obeyed.

ACKNOWLEDGMENTS

Contemporary Haibun Online
"Church Door Shadow" (Issue 16.3)
"Wrong Side of the Tracks" (Issue 17.1 and *Red Moon Press 17*)
"Transient" (Issue 17.3)
"Reinvention" (Issue 18.1)
"No Strings Attached" (Issue 18.3)

Drifting Sands Haibun
"Wear Your Best Black" (Issue 5)
"The Sayer of Grace" (Issue 7)
"Table for One" (Issue 8)
"The Hollow" (Issue 11)
"Tinseltown" (Issue 14)
"Catch and Release" (Issue 16)
"Ancient Stories" (Issue 16—contest winner)
"Inside Ingredient" (Issue 16—contest winner)
"Between the Bars" (Issue 17)

Filibuster (Auburn University of Montgomery 2012)
"Shoeshine in Tokyo"

Last Leaves Magazine
"Rearview" (October 2022 issue)

Poetry Quarterly
"Catacombs" (Summer 2019)
"Through the Lens" (Summer 2019)
"The Last of Their Kind" (Winter 2019)
"No Place to Call Home" (Spring 2020)
"Where the Lost Things Go" (Spring 2020—Rebecca Lard Award winner)

ACKNOWLEDGMENTS

"Loneliness" (Summer 2020)
"Inside the Globe" (Spring 2021—Rebecca Lard Award runner-up)

The Phoenix (Issue 64)
"Unmentionables"

San Antonio Review
"Write for Me" (October 2022)

Stone Poetry Quarterly
"Just for the Night" (November 2022 issue)

Voices of the Valley Clark State
"Rows Not Planted" (Issue 4)

ABOUT THE AUTHOR

Arvilla Fee has been married for over twenty years to Colonel James Fee and has six beautiful biological and adopted children (Kara, Kyle, Armoni, Jennica, Alec, and D'Andre), an amazing daughter-in-law, Stephanie, and sweet little granddaughter, Embree, all of whom she counts as her greatest blessings. She has had a long academic career, receiving a Bachelor's in the Science of Education from IUPUI, a Master's in Education from Weber State, and a Master's in Liberal Arts English from Auburn University of Montgomery. She has taught English in middle schools, high schools, and colleges, including her current position as an English adjunct at Clark State College. She has been published by numerous presses including *Poetry Quarterly, Inwood Indiana, 50 Haikus, Contemporary Haibun Online, Drifting Sands Haibun, Voices of the Valley, Acorn, Last Leaves Magazine, Bright Flash Literary Review, Stone Poetry Quarterly* and many others. She also won the Rebecca Lard Award for best poem in the Spring 2020 issue of *Poetry Quarterly* and won first place for two poems in the *Drifting Sands Haibun* contest in 2022.

What Arvilla loves most about writing is its kinetic energy—the ability to make people feel something. She believes that poetry, especially, packs the biggest emotional punch in the tiniest package. She often writes about the grittier side of life, which is the basis for this collection. Arvilla lost a sister-in-law to a drug overdose in 2014, a brother-in-law to a hit-and-run driver in 2016, and two step-parents to cancer in 2016 and 2017. Additionally, she has witnessed the trauma some of her students have endured and has been their most fierce advocate for success. She has also had firsthand experience with abuse, divorce, and a miscarriage. Through her husband's Air Force career, Arvilla has traveled the globe, observing cultures and the common struggles of humanity in places such as Japan, Germany, France, Belgium, Romania, Italy, Luxembourg, Switzerland, and Australia. For Arvilla, poetry has

ABOUT THE AUTHOR

never been about gaining elite literary status but about being in the trenches with ordinary people who will say, "She gets me."

www.ingramcontent.com/pod-product-compliance
Lightning Source LLC
Chambersburg PA
CBHW062221080426
42734CB00010B/1976